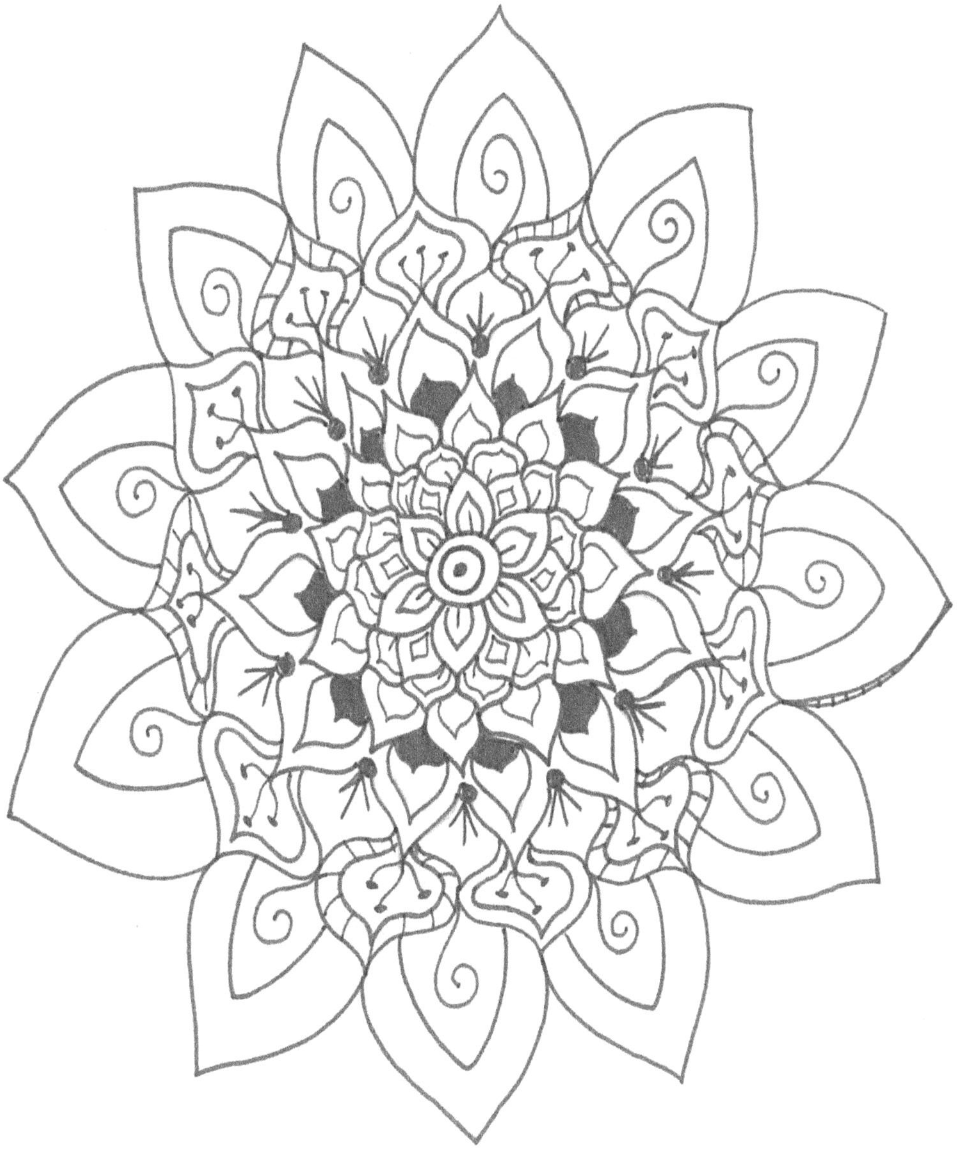

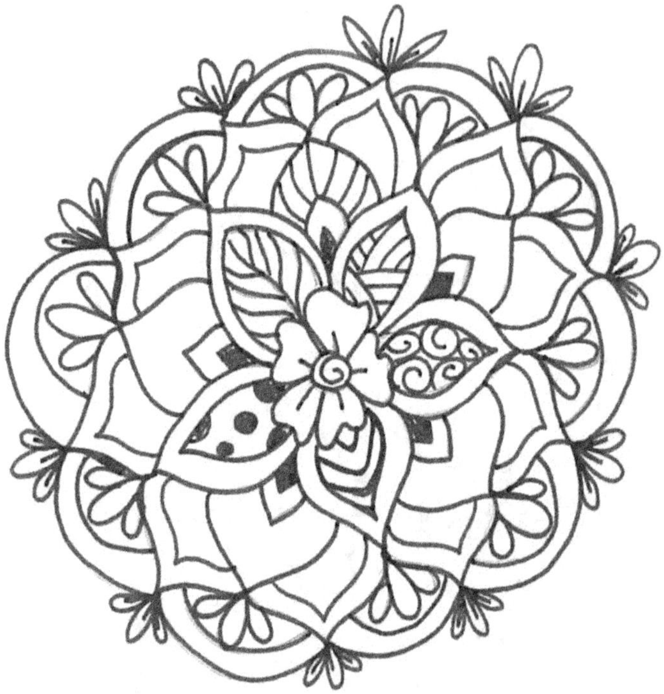

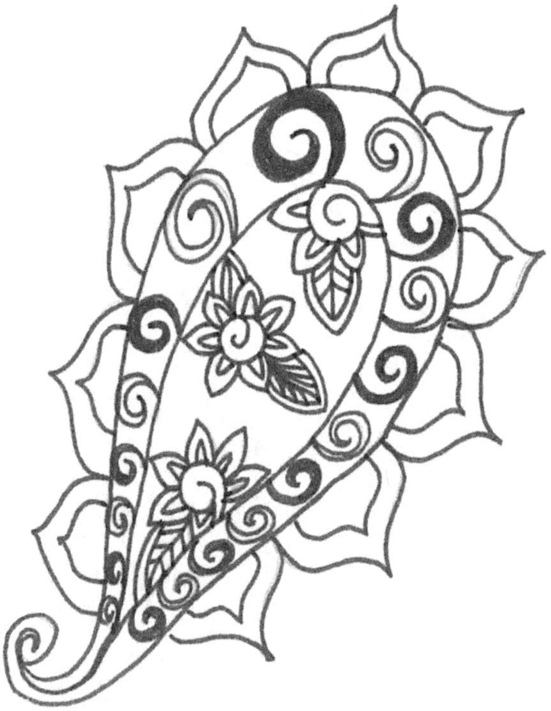

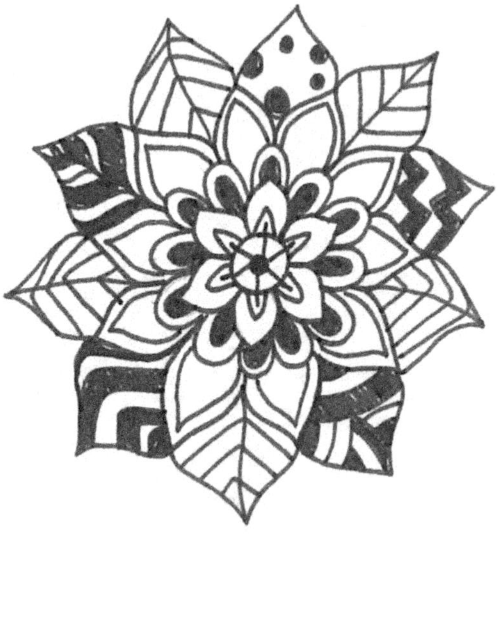

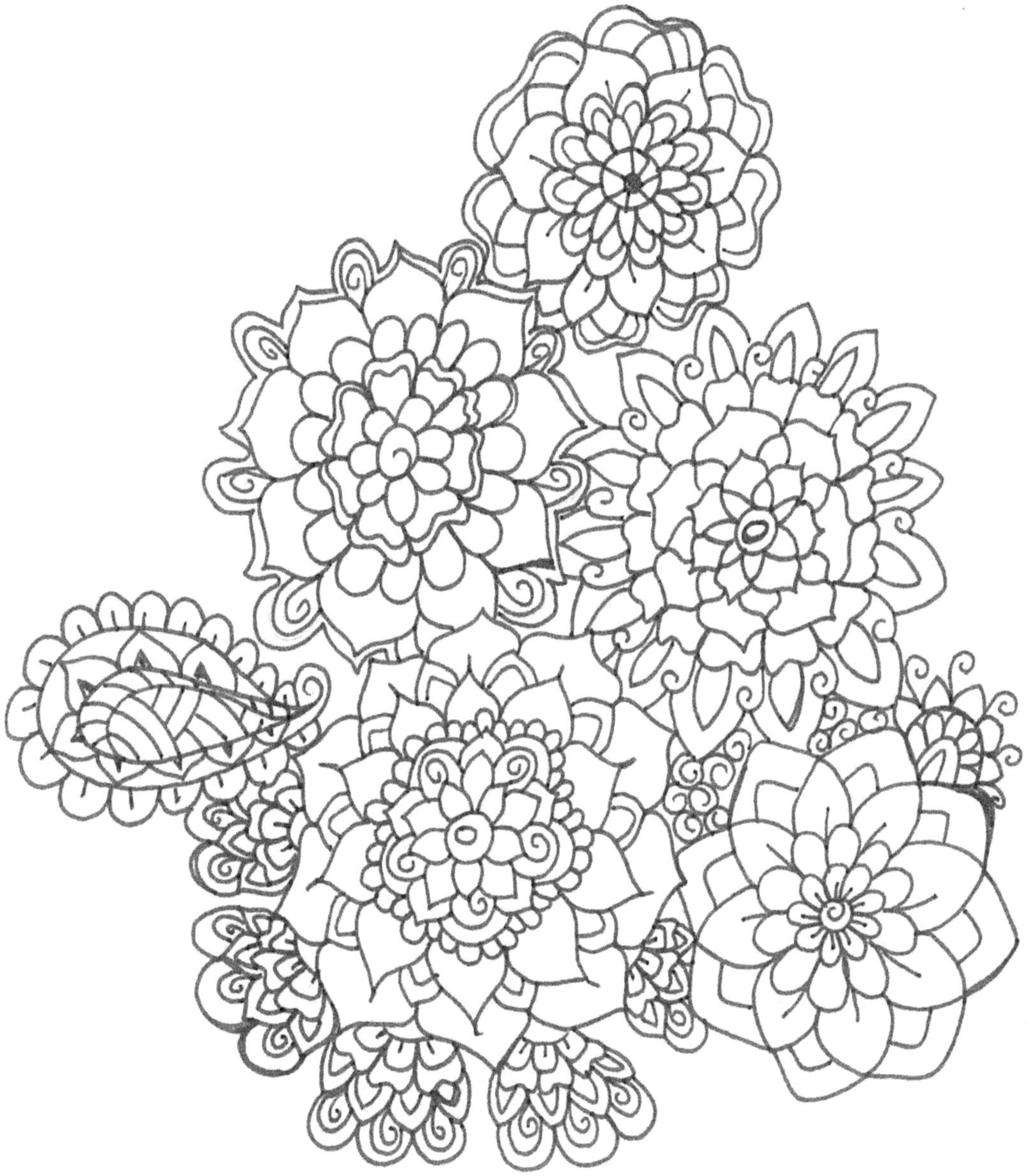

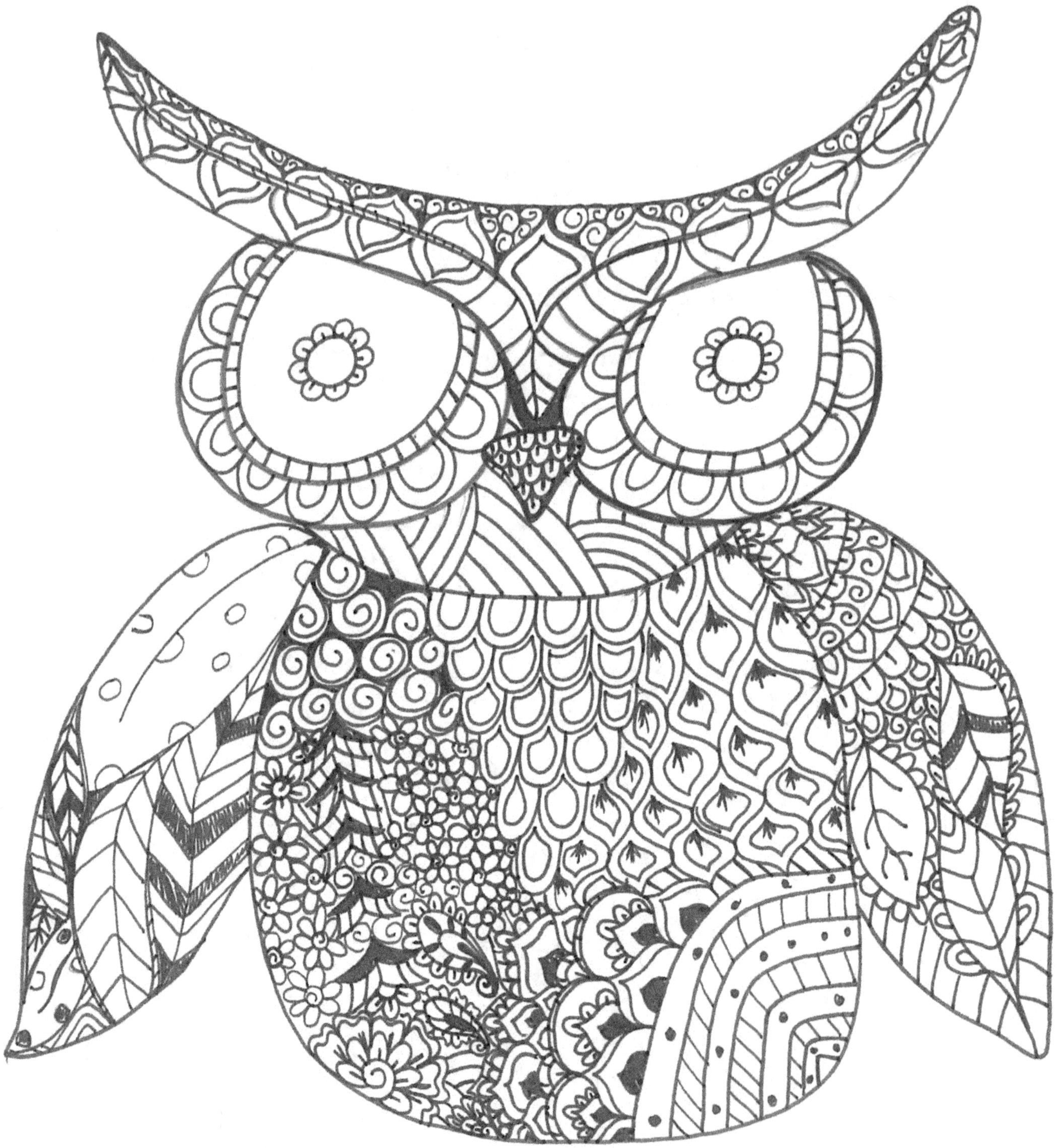

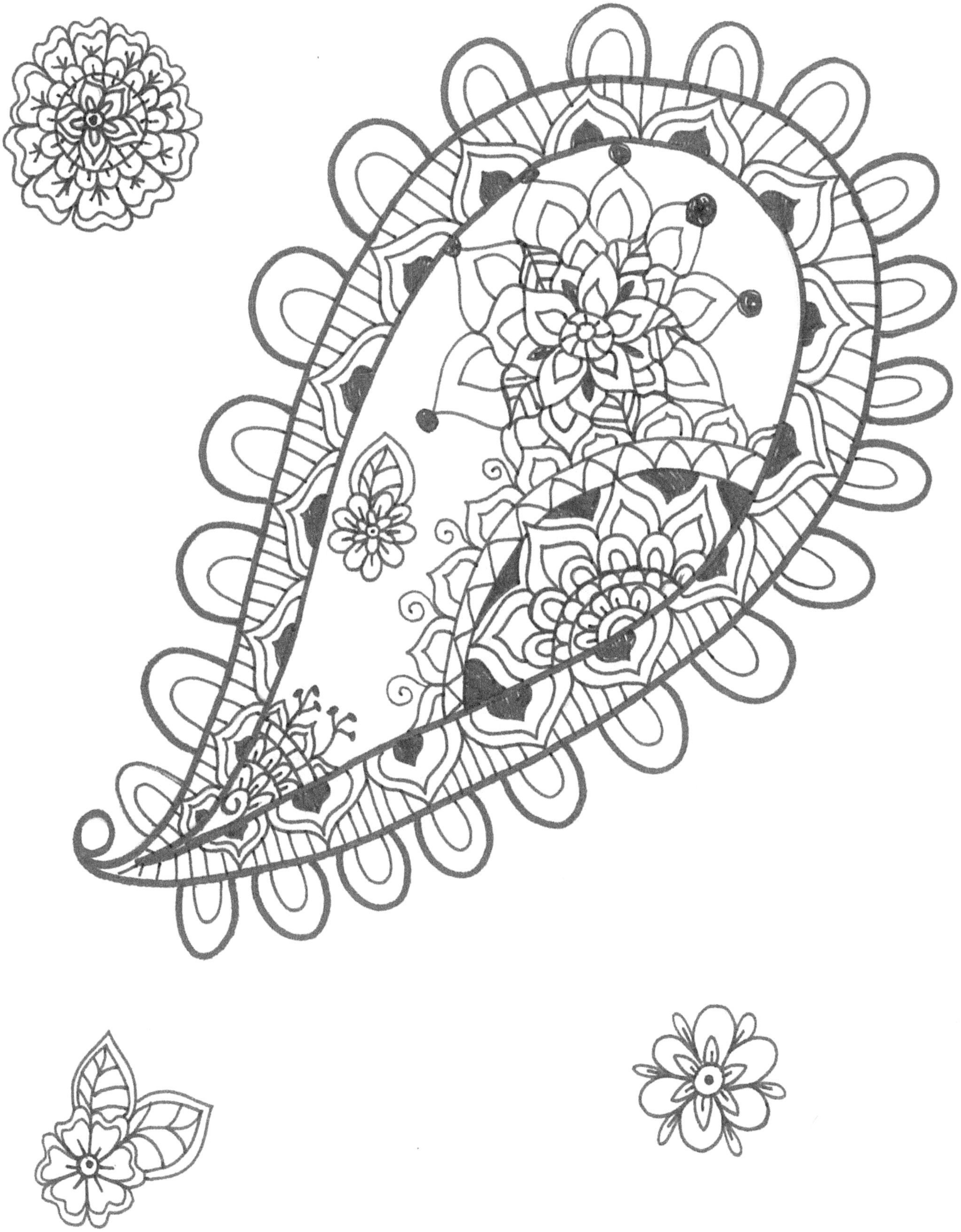

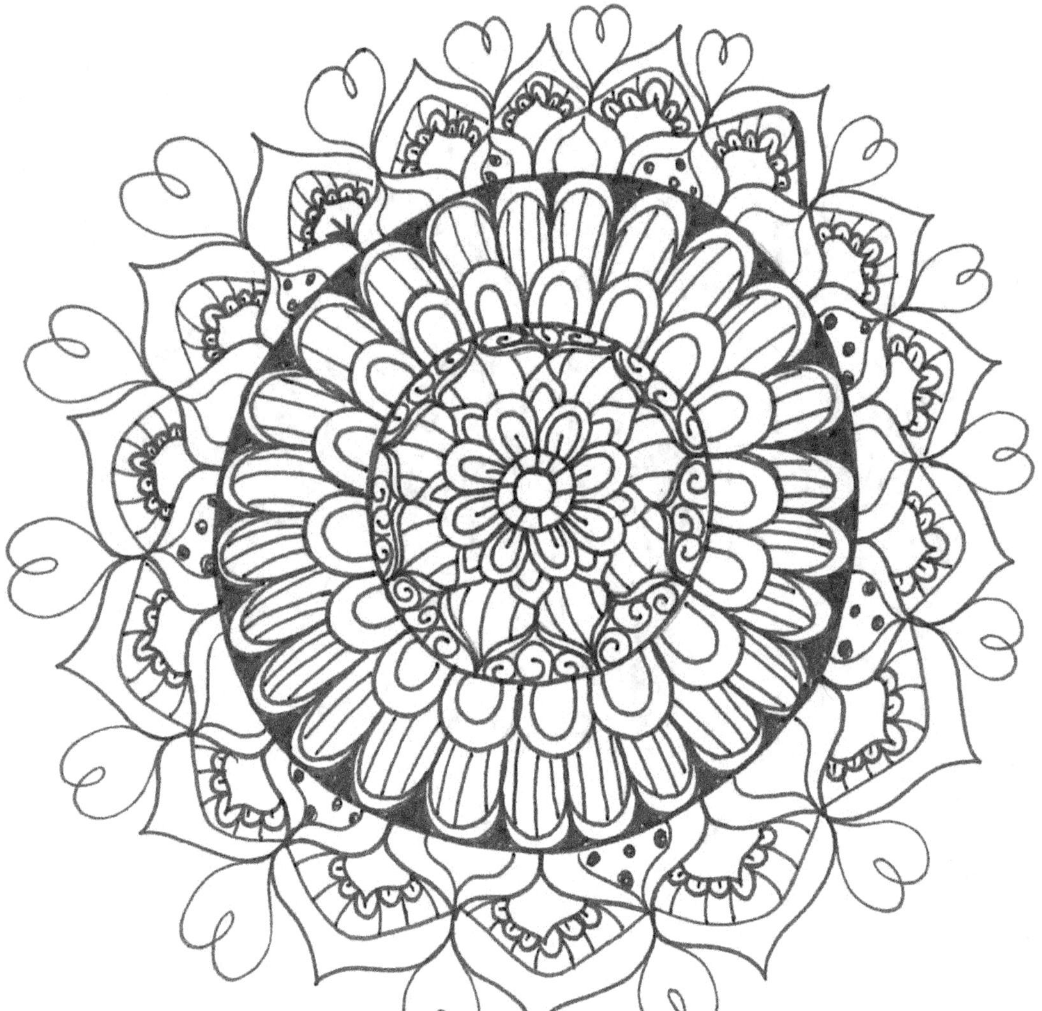

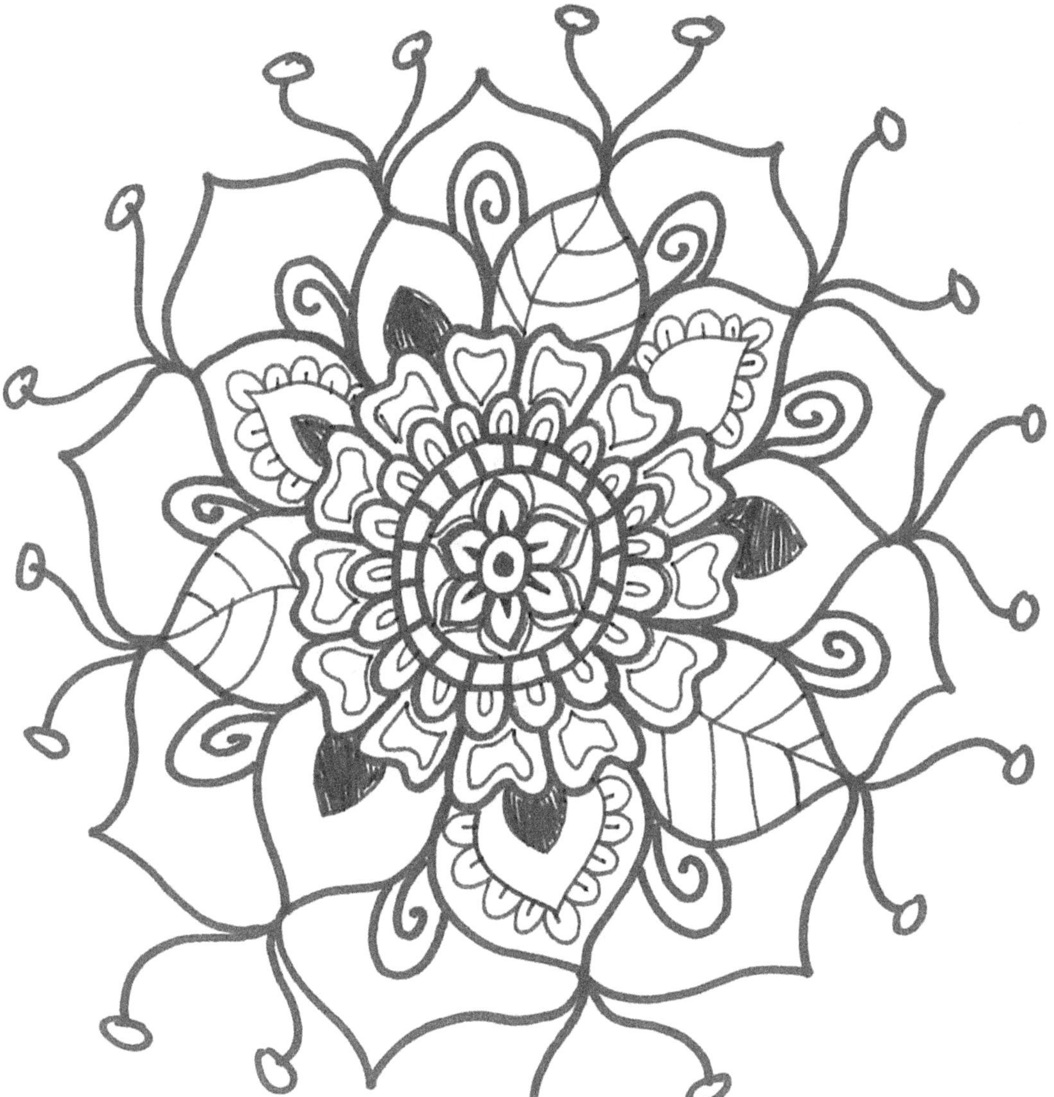

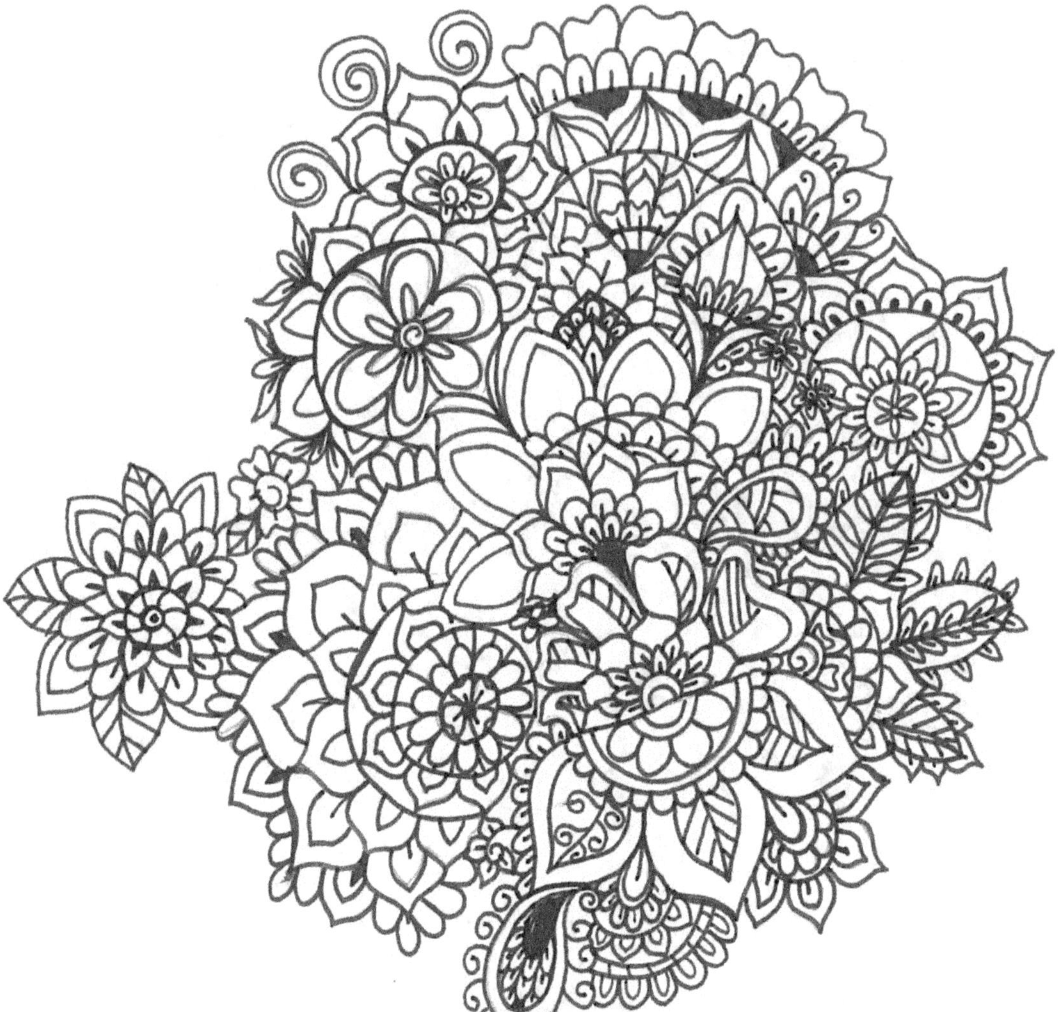

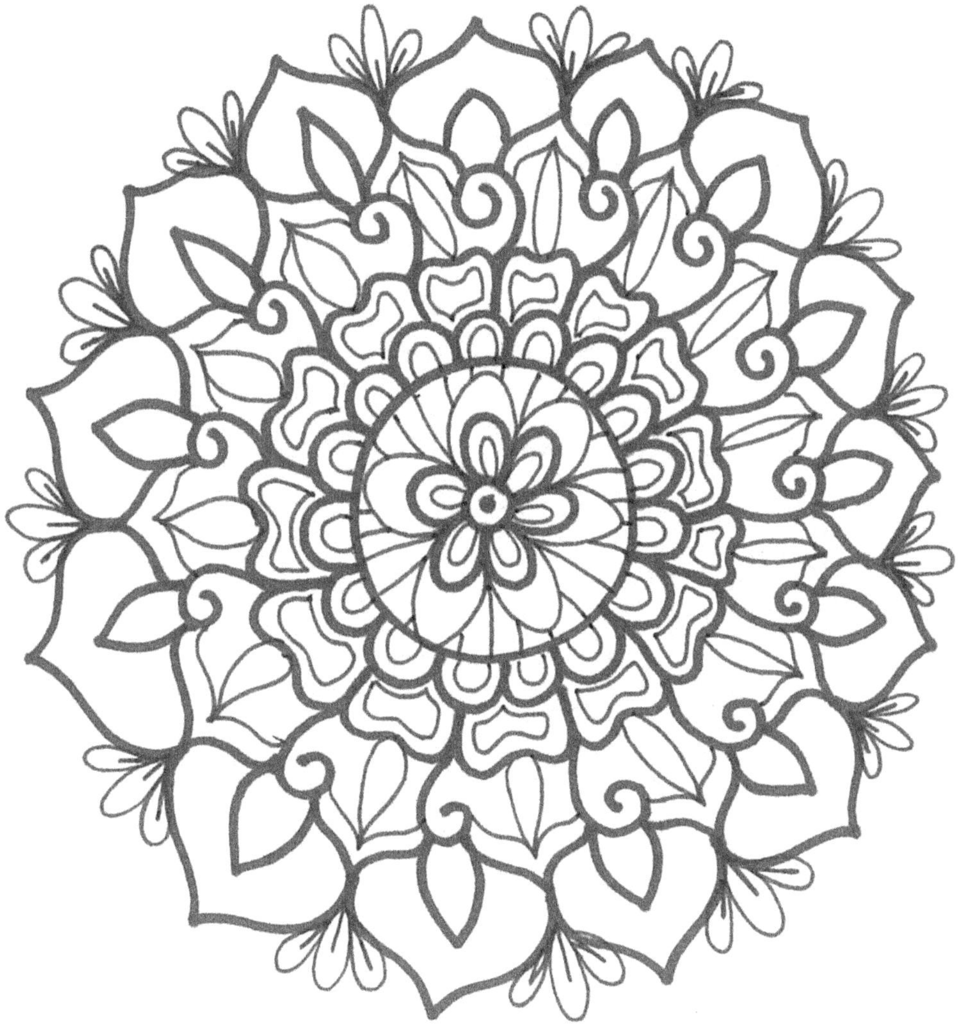

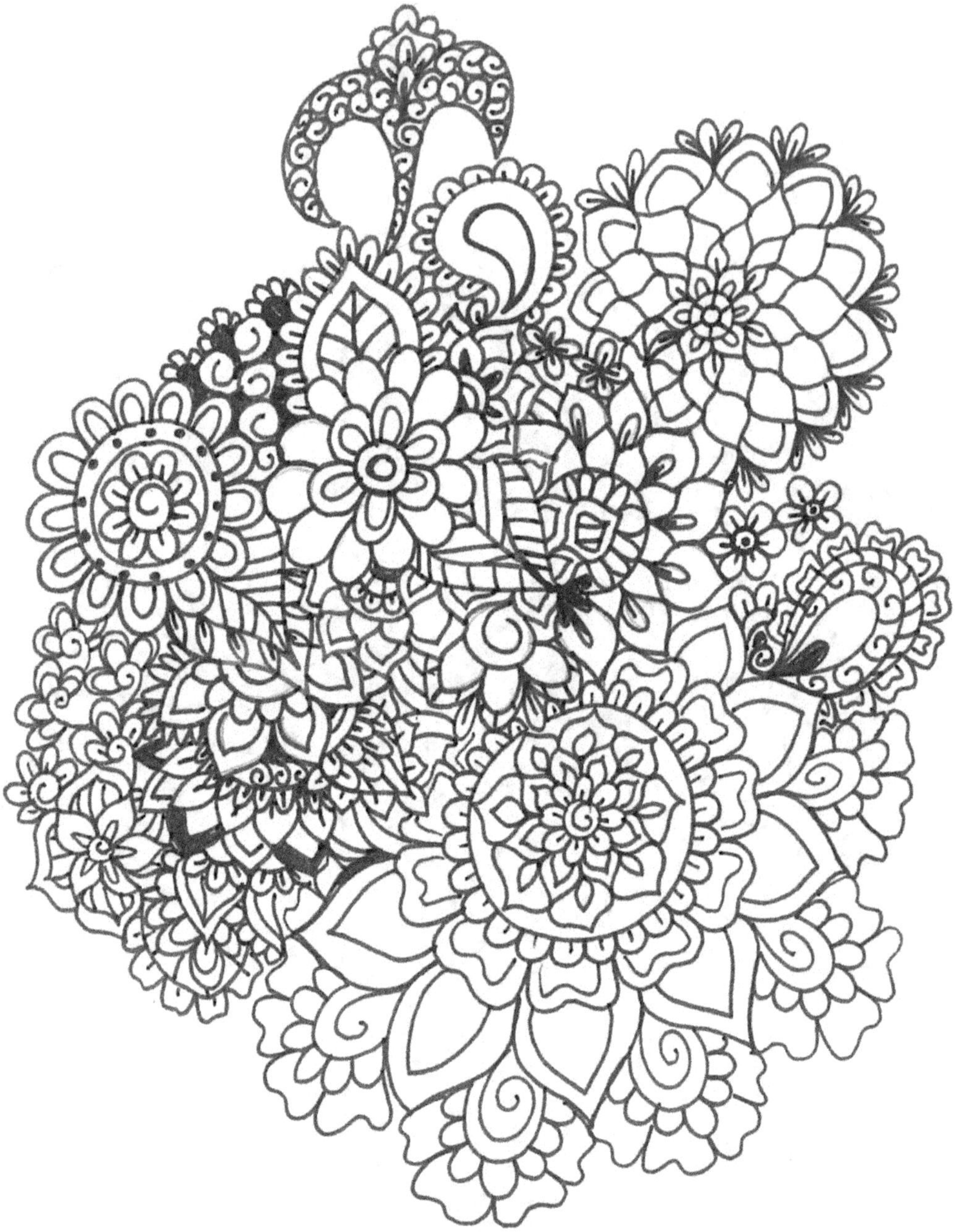

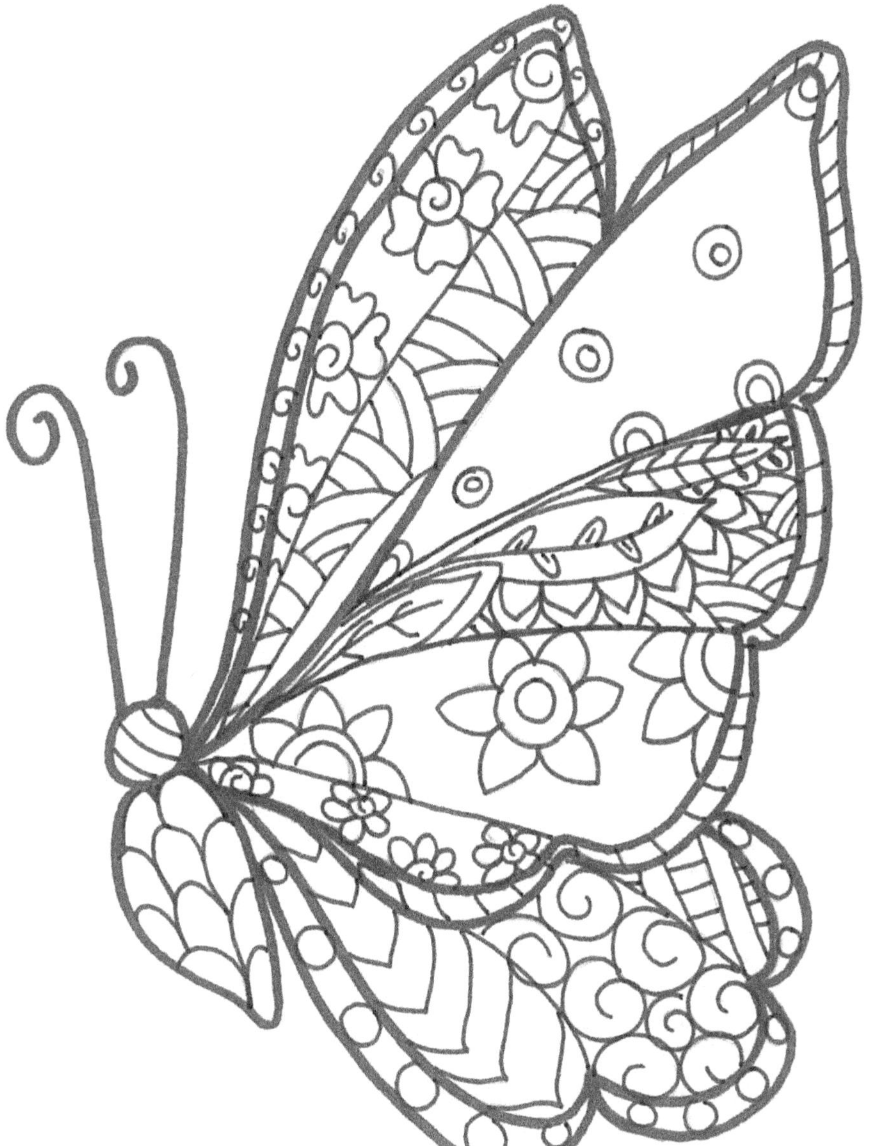

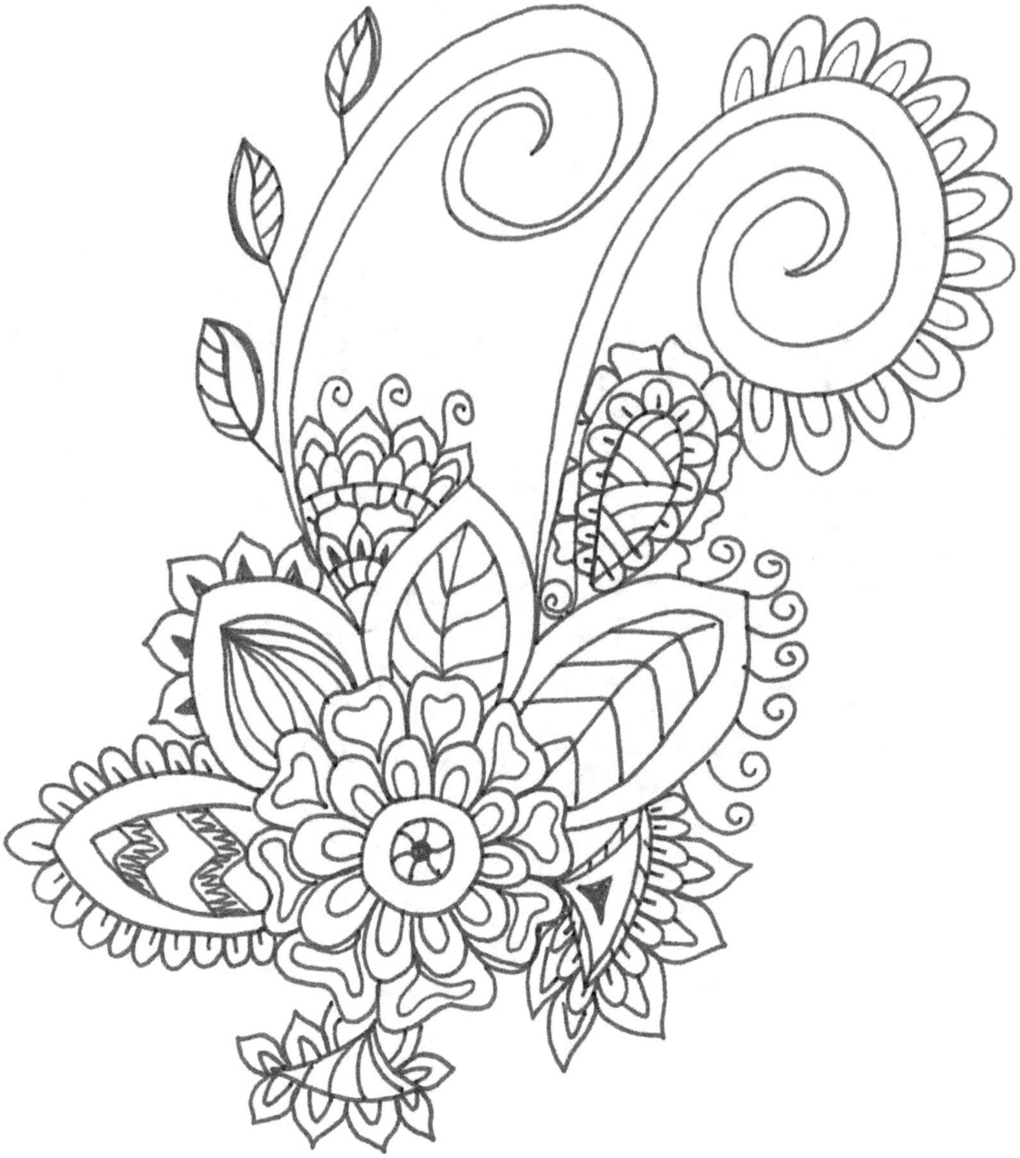

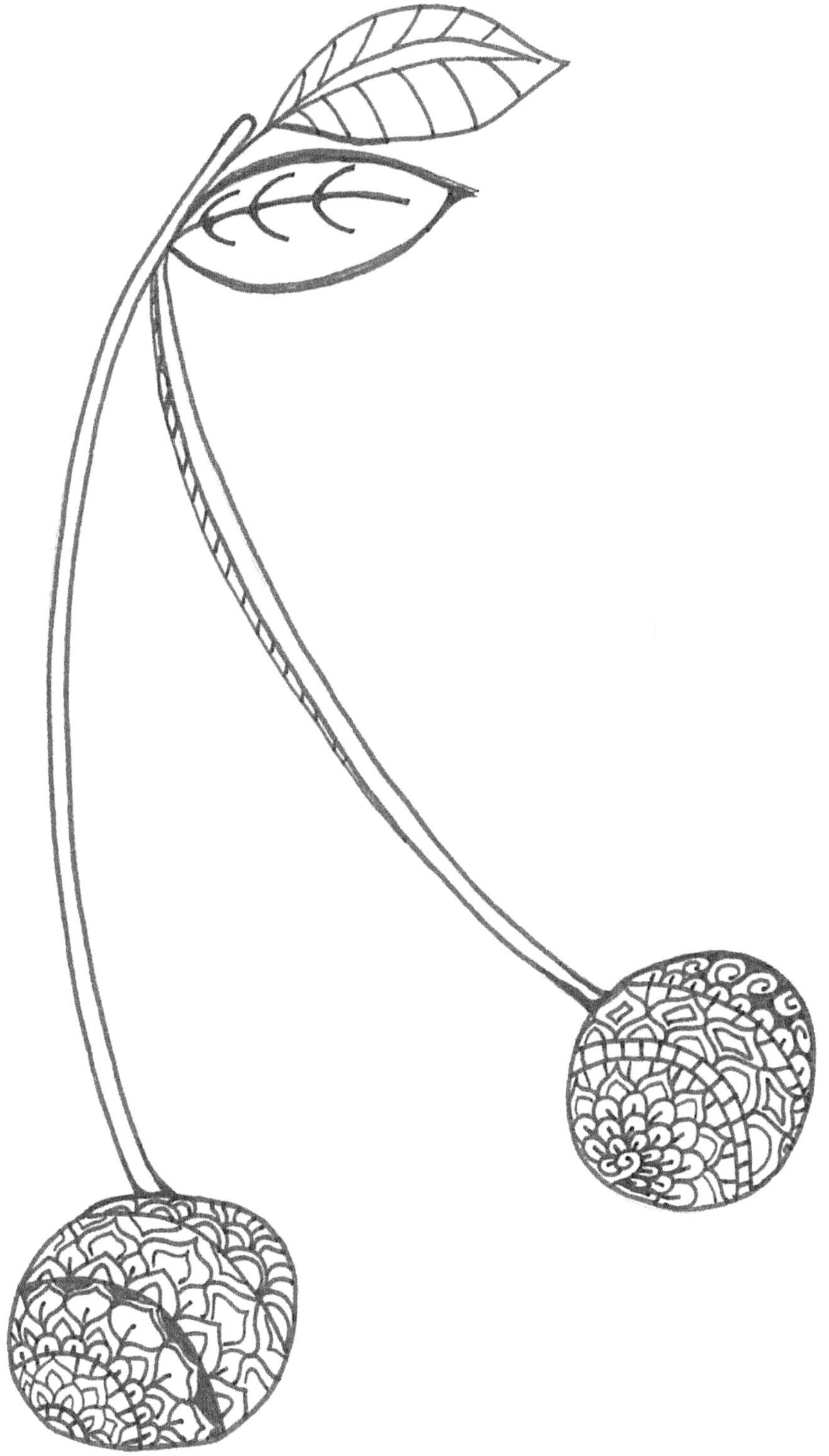

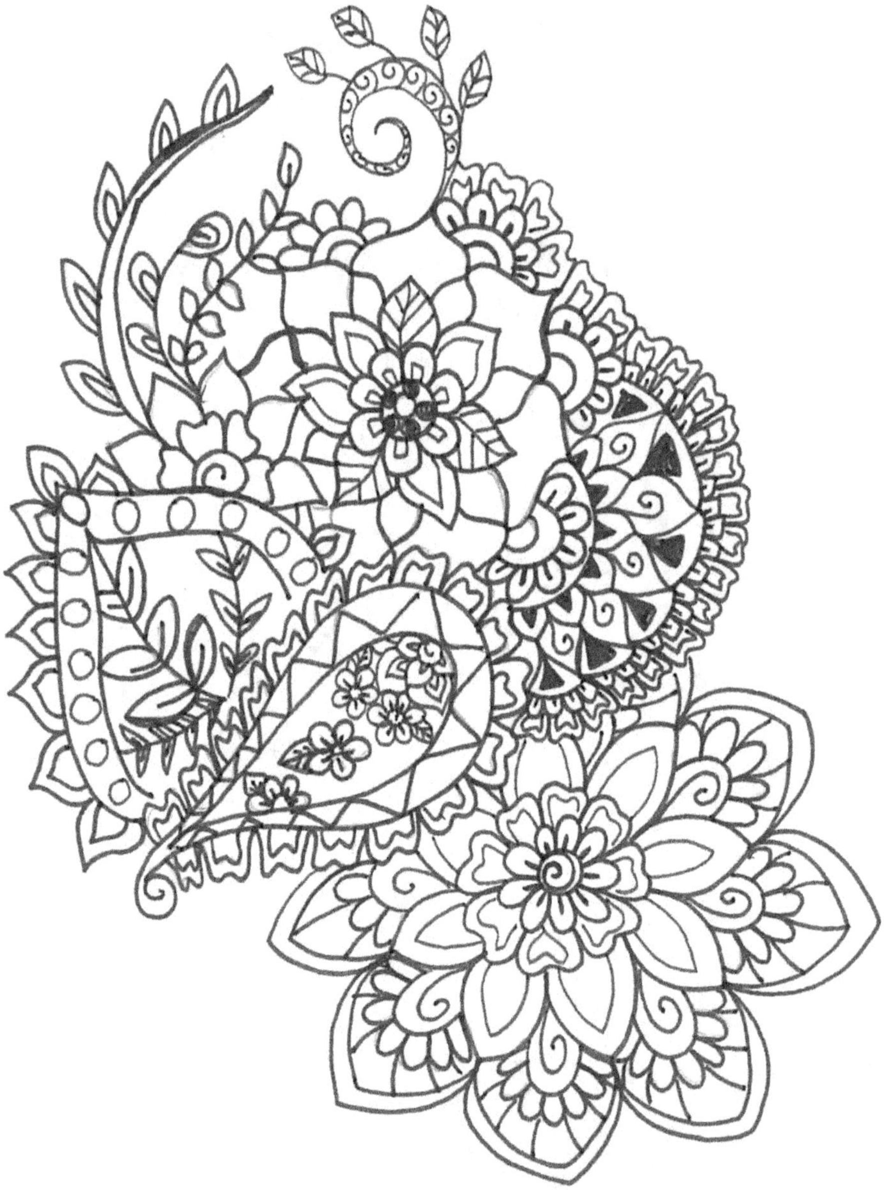

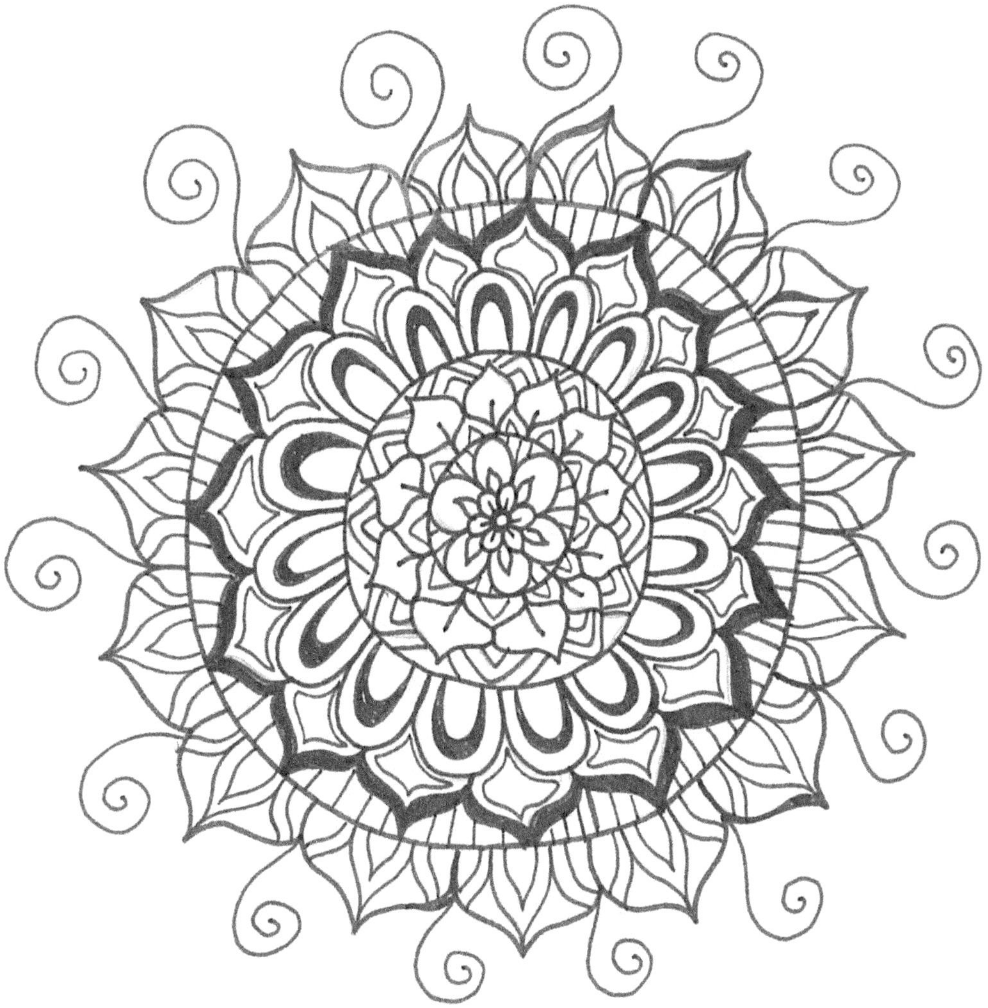

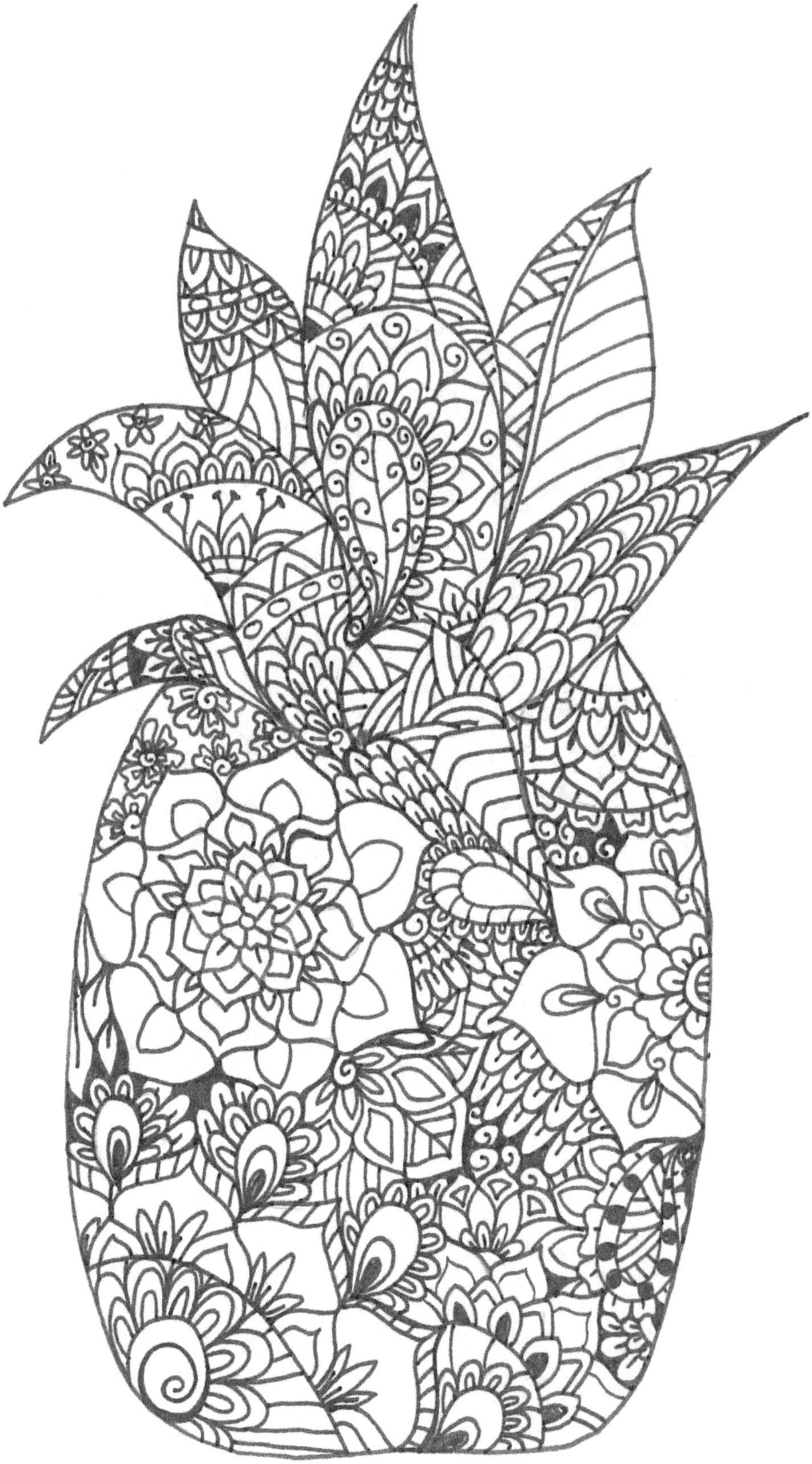

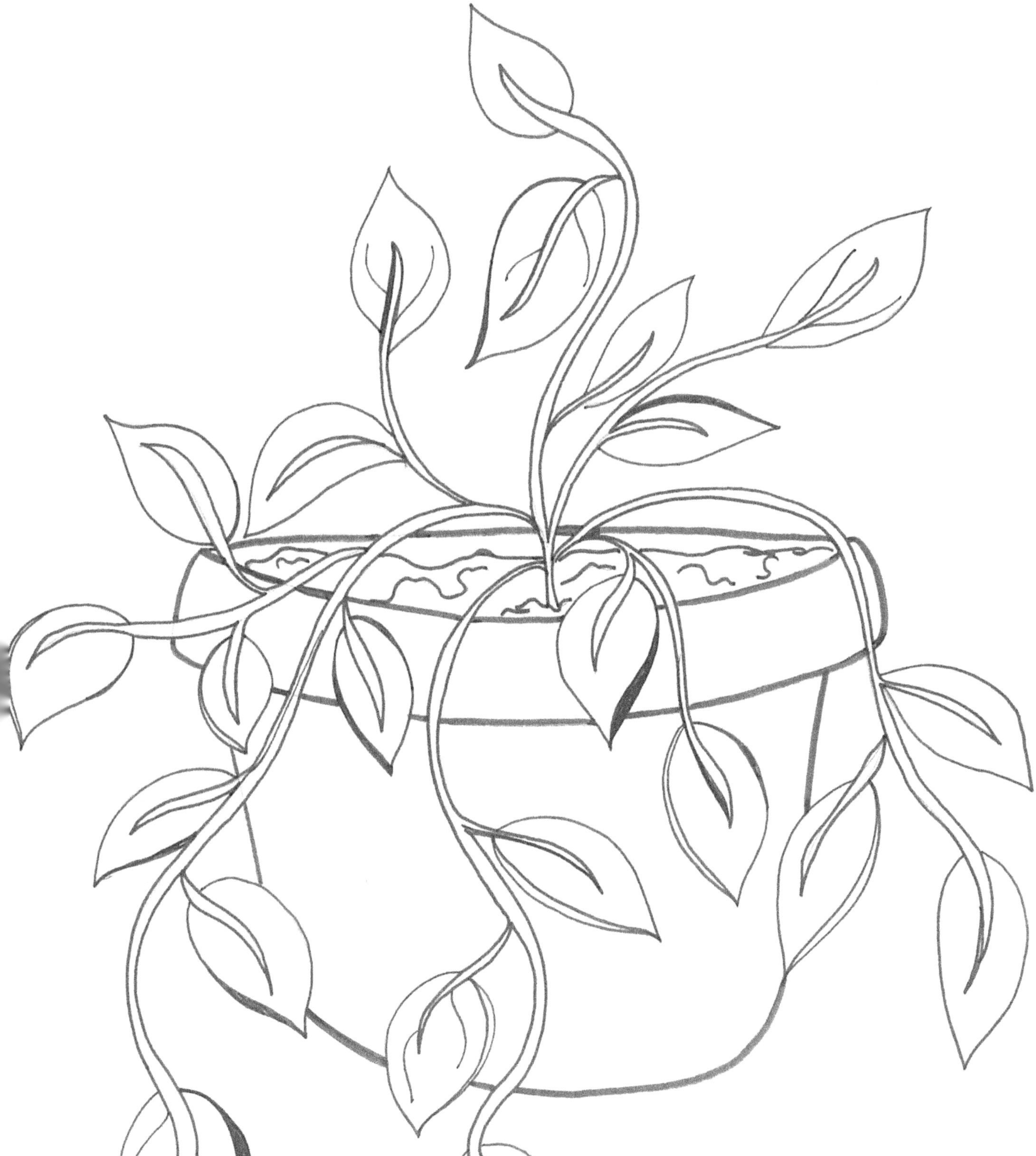

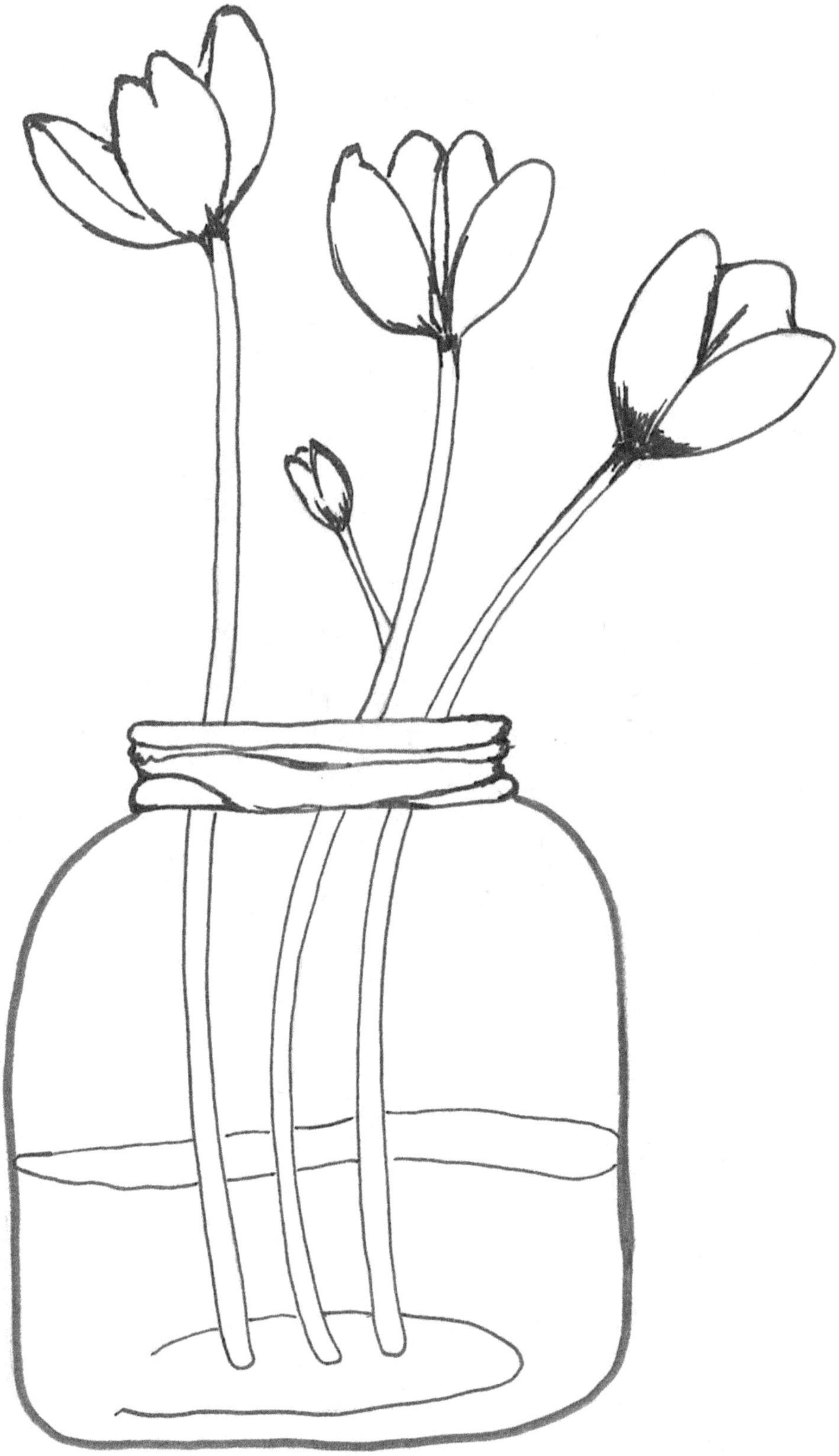

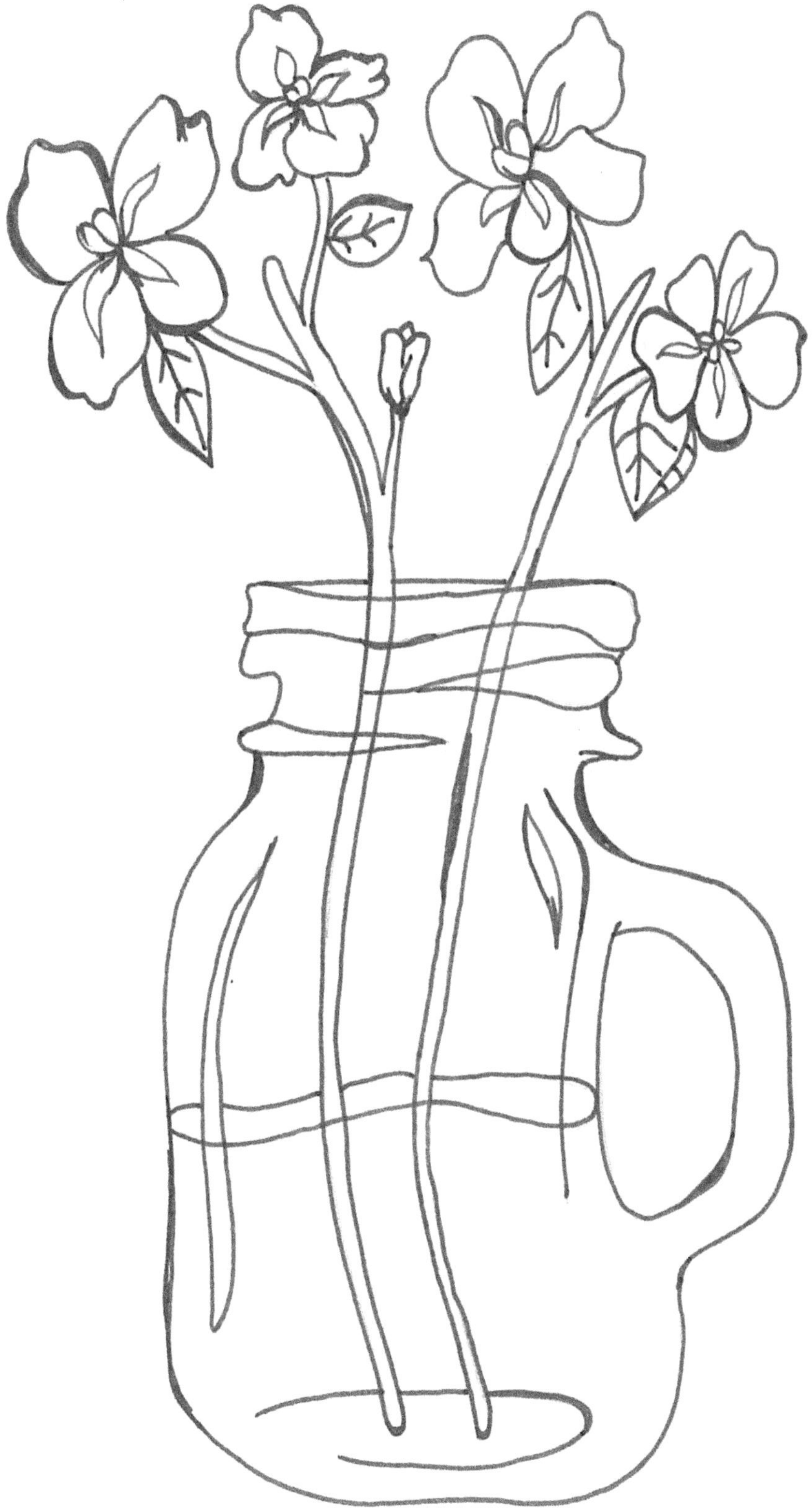

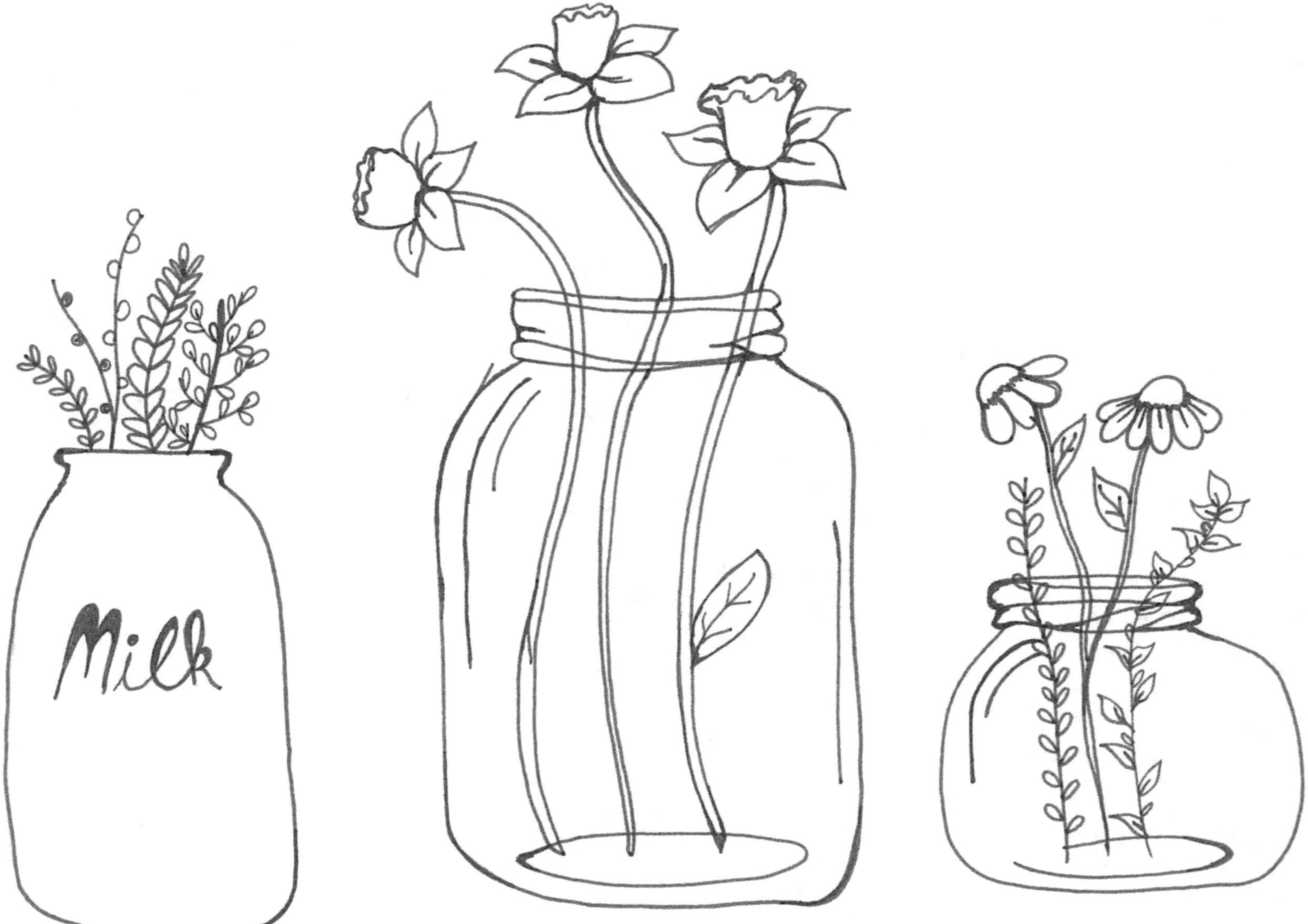
Milk

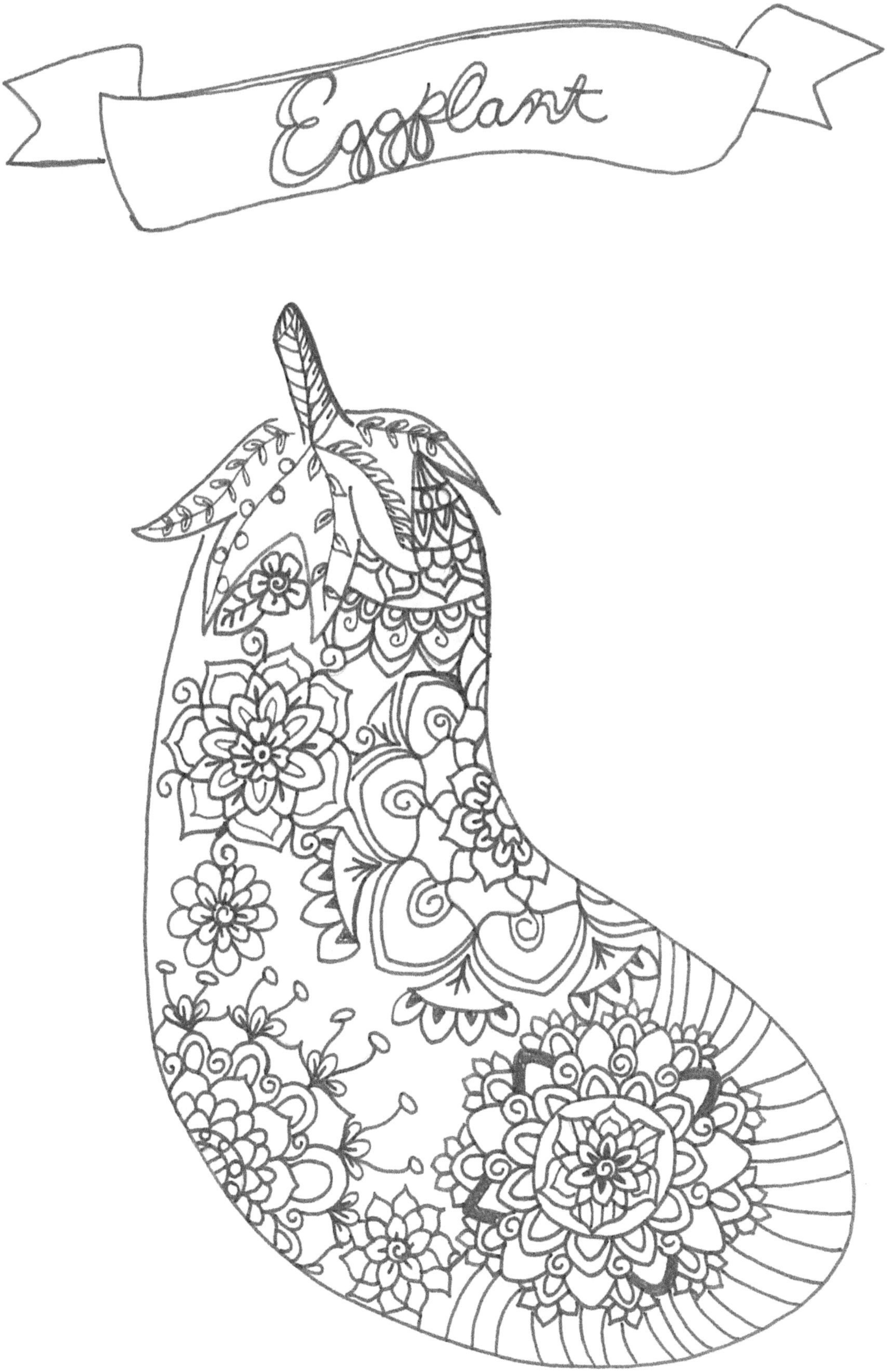
Eggplant

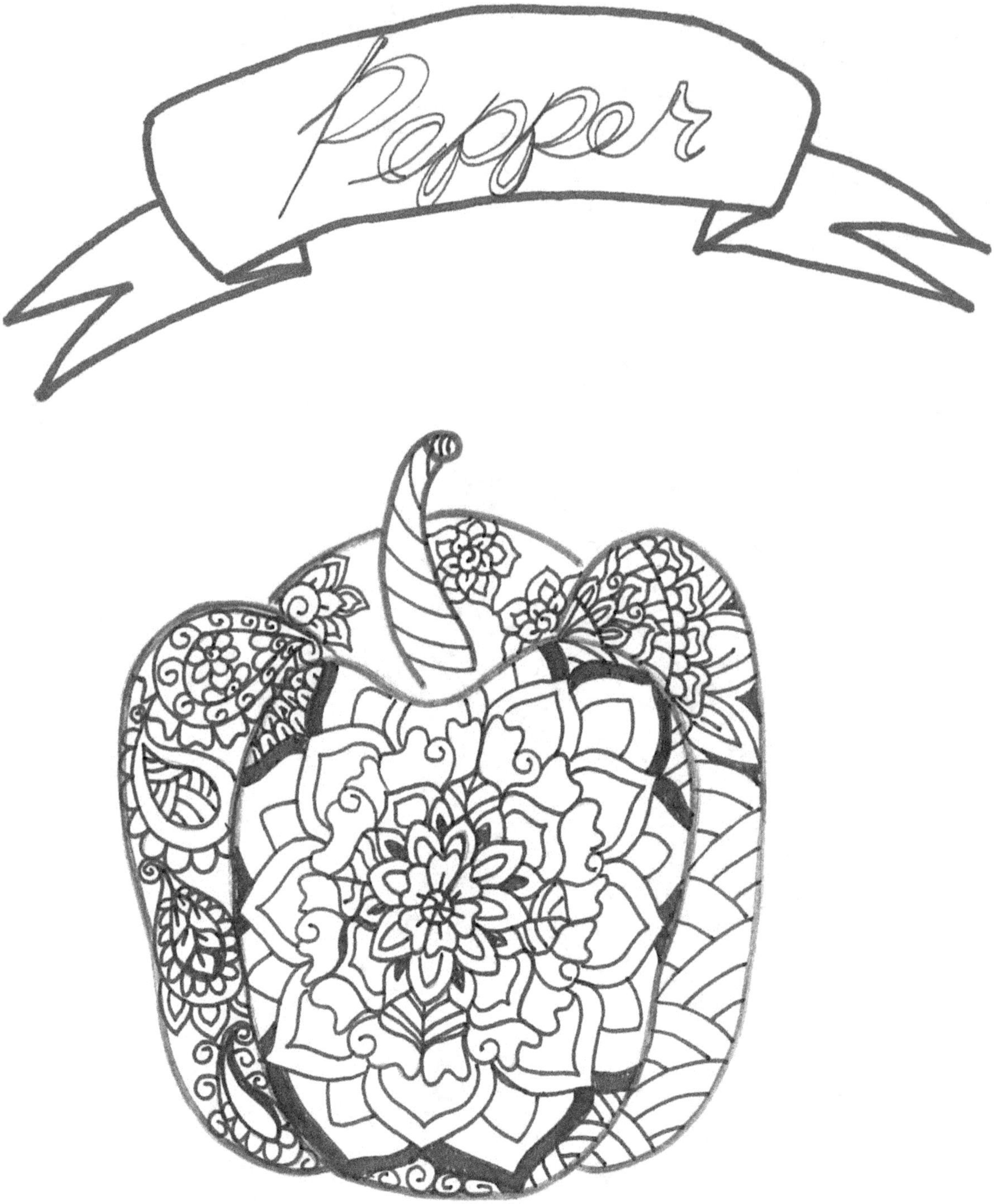
Pepper

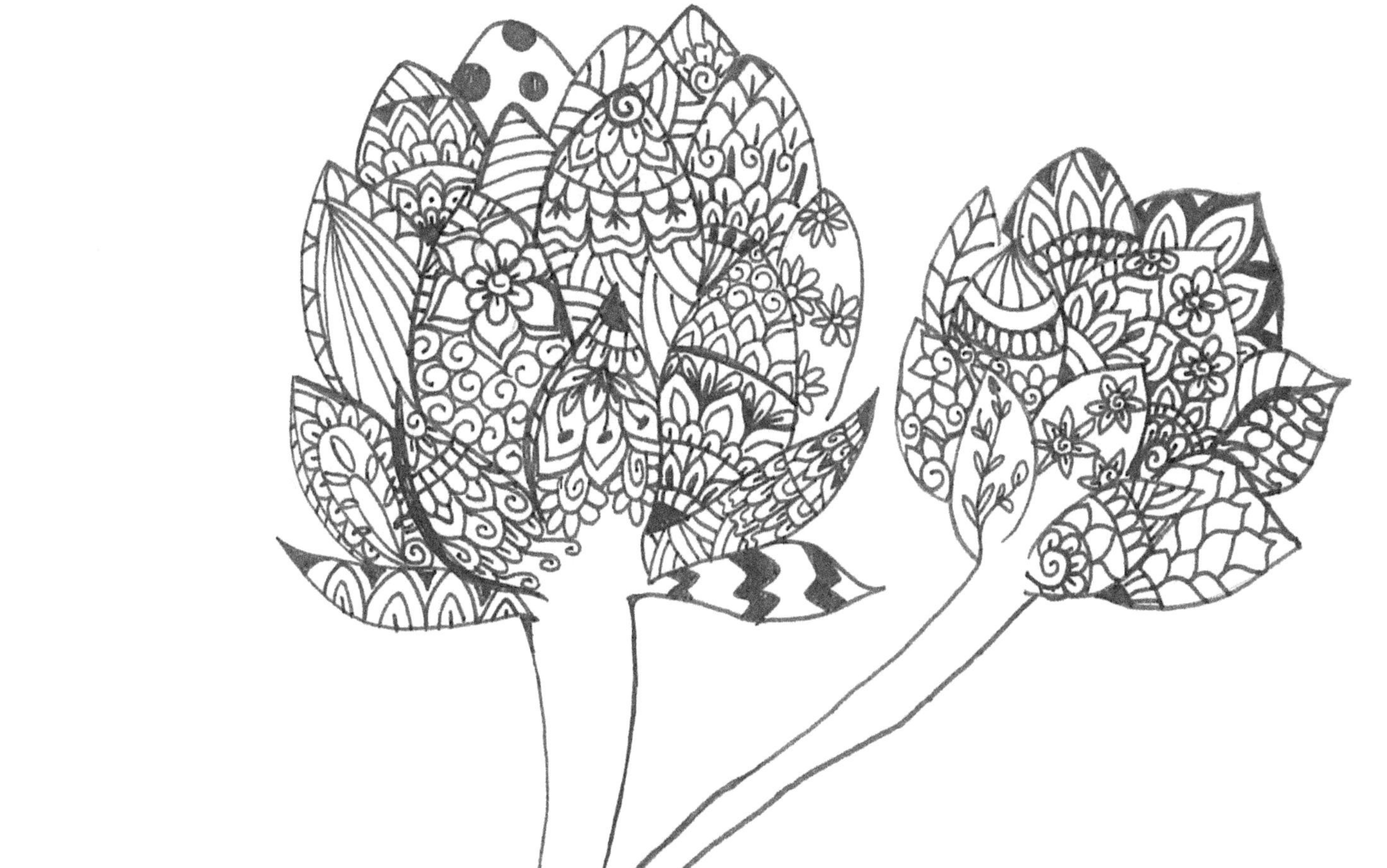
Artichokes

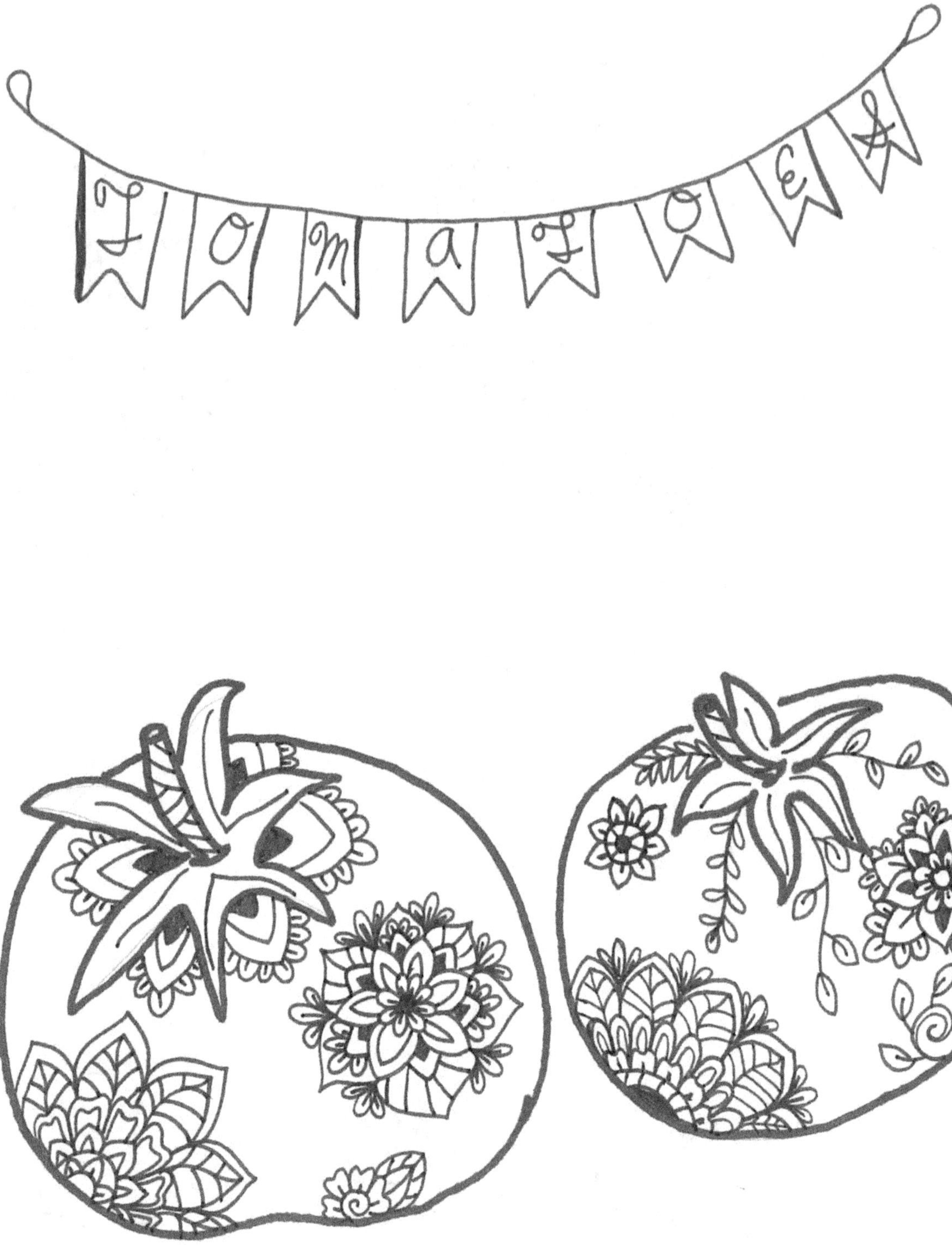
Tomatoes

www.ingramcontent.com/pod-product-compliance
Lightning Source LLC
Chambersburg PA
CBHW062238220526
45471CB00009B/3536
* 9 7 8 1 9 8 7 7 9 3 8 5 7 *